THE BLUEPRINT FOR MENTAL TOUGHNESS:

Becoming Emotionally Fit & Socially Responsible for The Game of Life!

THE BLUEPRINT FOR MENTAL TOUGHNESS JEMIAH BATTLE

JEMIAH BATTLE

The Blueprint for Mental Toughness

Published by Renaj Publishing

 Printed in the United States of America. For information and inquiries address Renaj Publishing, P.O. Box 24161, Greenville, S.C, 29616.

Cataloging-in-Publication data for this book is available from the library of Congress.

ISBN-13: **978-0692401545**

ISBN-10: **0692401547**

Renaj Publishing books are available at special discounts for bulk purchases in the U.S. by corporations, institutions, and other organizations. Please contact for more information.

About The Author

Jemiah Battle, aka Mr. EQ, is founder of The SELF Initiative, an Emotional fitness trainer, and certified life coach specializing in EQ, Identity Development , leadership development, and social & life transitions. This book is based on the tested, results-focused strategies that he uses daily with private clients and in his own life and relationships. He believes in real world Solutions for real world people. Jemiah is a sought after keynote speaker and media contributor. He coaches students, young professionals, athletes, celebrities, and high achievers in becoming emotionally fit, mentally tough, and socially responsible. He lives in Greenville, SC with his wife Renea, and has two kids. Jaheim & Maji.

You can follow him at:

www.Facebook.com/MrEQfitness

www.Twitter.com/MrEQfitness

Instagram @MrEQfitness

To learn more about him and his initiatives visit WWW.JemiahBattle.com

Table of Contents

“I CAN’T MAKE YOU A CHAMPION, BUT I CAN TEACH YOU HOW TO THINK LIKE ONE!”

-JIM FANNIN

Mental Toughness

Life, Careers, and Sports should be an adventure, to be savored from beginning to end. They both are a game of constantly changing odds, constantly developing challenges, constantly opening opportunities.

Throughout this workbook there will be a scannable QR code at the end of each major section that will send you to a motivational video that will engage you. If you don't have a QR scanner on your smart phone or tablet here are some links to download them: (www.qrstuff.com), (https://scan.me/download), or you can visit your App Store on ITunes, Google Play, or The Microsoft Store. This workbook is for you!

You have to: **Take your development and achievement seriously!**

To win either, you have to play. Sitting on the sidelines won't do. Even after you've achieved all you ever hoped to achieve, it's no time to stop living. This requires "mental toughness."

MENTAL TOUGHNESS: Having the ability to be mentally tough enough to make the right personal, social and professional decisions is mental toughness outside of the sporting context. Most athletes are controlled by their urges, instincts and unrealistic desires. Having the ability to be mentally tough enough to take control of their urges, instincts and unrealistic desires is learned over time. Like attending class but not mentally prepared, making the decision not to attend the frat party the night before a game, studying for a test days before not the night before, keeping your cool when having a disagreement with your girlfriend, having the ability to leave your entitlement ego in your dorm room while on campus are just a few of the areas of mental toughness in action.

Preparing the mind for any type of endeavor consists of several aspects—coming to terms with what lays ahead is a good start. After that it's probably a good idea to consider setting goals and mapping out exactly how you plan to achieve them. This should ease anxiety by providing manageable steps to make the desired outcomes seem much more attainable. In addition, it's critical for any successful athlete to begin the process of mental strengthening. This can be done by constantly reminding yourself of the potential rewards waiting at the end of your hard work and dedication (motivation) while simultaneously conditioning the mind for long periods of constant pain-emotionally and physically. The mind can embrace this pain by blocking out as much of it as you can while also believing it's all worth it—for this to happen you must find a way to have fun whenever and however possible, and you must have a "why." A positive attitude can make all the difference in the world. Without any one of these essential elements, that player is sure to struggle mightily while trying to compete against the best athletes in the world.

4 Steps to Mental Toughness: Mentally Tough vs. Mentally Weak

1. **Attitude Change**
   Tough: Thinks, "I'll get the next one," remains positive and does not lose self-belief.
   Weak: Thinks, "I made a mess of that," becomes negative and loses self-belief.
2. **Emotional Response**
   Tough: Remains positive in direction and high in intensity.
   Weak: Becomes irritated and discouraged, loses hope and Blames others.
3. **Resultant Energy State**
   Tough: Remains positive in direction and high in intensity.
   Weak: Becomes negative in direction and high in intensity.
4. **Effect on Performance**
   Tough: Recovers well and makes good decisions later in the game.
   Weak: Becomes very nervous and hides in the game or situations, being more concerned with the past than the future.

To be mentally tough, being physically fit just isn't enough. It takes more than muscle. It takes more than sheer determination. It takes more than practice. You have to be socially & emotionally fit(tm) to really be the true leader that you are.

What is Social + Emotional Fitness?

SELF Fit = Know. Choose. Give.

"Emotional Fitness is the bridge between your dreams and your realities."

Emotional Intelligence is the capacity to create positive outcomes in relationship to others and ourselves. It is the practice of being aware, understanding, and appropriately expressing and handling emotional states. Skills in emotional intelligence can be practiced and developed at any point in your life.

Some recent Findings Examining The Impact of EQ

- **Higher achieving people demonstrated higher total EQ, Intrapersonal Skills, Stress Tolerance and Adaptability.**
- **People who are anxious or depressed get lower grades/lower achievement scores.**
- **People who respond to setbacks with hope and resilience vs. anger and hopelessness achieve higher academic and social success.**
- **Low levels of empathy are associated with poor achievement.**

Identity

Nothing is more powerful than the force of personal identity—when a person's soul transcends the limits of the moment to embrace all that they are capable of becoming.

- Anthony Robbins

Who are you? What ticks you off? What are your emotional triggers? What makes you happy? Why? Does those emotions serve or protect you? If not, do you still need to react that way?

"I AM" are the 2 most powerful words that you will ever say. Your purpose comes from your identity, and without identity we have no concrete purpose.

Take 60 seconds, 1 minute and just write 21 "I AM" statements:

I AM____

I AM____

I AM____

I AM____

I AM____

I AM____

I AM____

I AM____

I AM____

I AM____

I AM____

I AM____

I AM____

I AM____

I AM____

I AM____

I AM____

I AM____

I AM____

I AM____

I AM____

Was that difficult?

Anxiety comes from not having a proper self-identity. Anxiety comes when fear goes unchecked. Anxiety wants to attack you at your core, and who YOU believe you are. Anxiety is the worse pain because it leaves you lost in the moment. Anxiety paralyzes you. Knowing who you are is the antidote to anxiety.

Repeat after me,

"IF I KNOW WHO I AM, I KNOW HOW TO WIN BECAUSE I WIN AS ME!"

Your Best Self

What does it really mean to become your "best self"? What if you've never been this person before? What standard do you use to determine what characteristics to soot for? How do you know if you're aiming too high…or too low?

How do you even know who your best self is and how to become that person?

This workbook is going to lead you into becoming your best self and getting rid of the things and thoughts that are in the way. Think about this: becoming who you really are should never feel forced or awkward. Instead, it will feel completely natural in every way. You'll feel at home in your own skin. You'll no longer feel that you're an imposter who's trying to "fake it til' they make it."

But it starts with understanding the things which are keeping you from discovering your true self. Let's look at a few of them:

Other People's Opinions

Everyone has opinions about the way that things should be, and that's okay. But you should never feel that your life and your choices are at the mercy of other people's opinions. As you are reading this , you can probably think of at least a few people who have an opinion about who you should be or what you should do with your life.

Sometimes these opinions are negative, and sometimes they are positive. But one thing is for certain…

These opinions have nothing to do with who you really are.

They simply represent people who are realizing their own perception of you. At times, these opinions can be positive. But if they aren't a genuine representation of who you honestly believe that you are, they can be a hindrance towards you becoming your best self.

Imitation has never caused anyone to become great. It's ok to mock or model someone you admire and respect to master their skills and techniques, but at some point you have to trust who you really are and embrace your uniqueness and creativity. You're never going to be as good at being someone else as you can be at being yourself. You're not responsible for becoming anybody but the person you want to be, and that's a decision you, and only you, can make.

You are not responsible for other people's opinions or perceptions of you, whether those opinions and perceptions are good or bad. You are only responsible for being true to the best that is in you!

No matter who you become, for better or worse, somebody somewhere is always going to have negative opinion about it. That's not your problem to fix. It's their problem, and it's their responsibility...so leave it at that.

Your Weaknesses and Your doubts

Everyone has things about themselves which give them doubts, just as they have things which they are confident about. Everyone also has things which they don't do you so well, just as they have things that they do well. The person you become in life is dependent upon whether or not you focus on your strengths or your weaknesses. Being mentally tough is not being without weaknesses.

Yes it is important that you examine the areas of your character that you need to change in order to get what you want out of your life and optimize every opportunity, but it is better to focus on a specific plan of action for correcting the weakness than to focus on the weakness itself.

Think of it like this: If you're constantly focusing on making your weaknesses and insecurities or feeling ashamed, it's as if you are placing a magnifying glass over them. As this happens, they become the predominating thoughts in your mind until they begin to affect your self-image and your beliefs. Those beliefs affect your actions and those actions create your results and your lifestyle.

Sound familiar?

And in case you're wondering whether or not other people recognize this, they do. In fact, it's probably more obvious than you think it is. That's the bad news.

The good news is that your strengths are the same way. If you're constantly focusing on developing the strong points of character, it's as if you are placing a magnifying glass over them. As this happens, they become the dominating thoughts in your mind and they begin to form your self-image and your beliefs.

These beliefs begin to influence your actions, and those actions reinforce your beliefs and create your lifestyle and identity.

And the final things which keep you from knowing and becoming your best self...

Your Current Results

As you're considering the fact that your thought create your beliefs and your self-image, that your beliefs influence your actions, and that you're actions form your lifestyle and identity, it might be easy to feel bad about yourself if you're not happy with your current results. We will go into depth about this even more in the workbook in the section.

It's important to remember that the current circumstances of your life are a representation of who you were, not who you are. If you begin today to focus on becoming a different person, you can be certain that your current results will change, but first you have to let go of the idea that those results represent who you are.

In fact, it's important that you don't ever allow the exterior circumstances of your life to define your self-image and identity. If you do, your self-image and confidence will vacillate just as the circumstances of your life do. Better to develop a rock solid self-image based on a standard which you and you alone determine.

This will help you to endure the difficulty in your life and keep your actions consistent with your true values instead of allowing them to be influenced by circumstances.

You & Your Character

Personal success is built on the foundation of character, and **character is the result of hundreds and hundreds of choices you might make that gradually turn who you are at any given moment into who you want to be.** If that decision-making process is not present, you'll still be somebody—you'll still be alive—but you may have a personality rather than a character, and to me that's something very different.

Character isn't something you were born with and can't change, like your fingerprints. It's something you must take responsibility for forming. **You build character by how you respond to what happens in your life**, whether it's winning every game, losing every game, getting rich or dealing with hard times. Your character is not who you are when no one is looking. Your character is the permanent impression that you leave on others.

You build character from certain qualities that you must create and diligently nurture within yourself, just like you would a plant and water a seed or gather wood to build a campfire. You've got to look for those things in your heart and in your gut. You've got to chisel away in order to find them, just like chiseling away rock to create the sculpture that has previously existed only in the imagination.

But the really amazing thing about character is that if you're sincerely committed to making yourself into the person you want to be, you'll not only create those qualities, you'll strengthen them and recreate them in abundance. Building your character is vital to becoming all you can be.

Getting to SELF-ACTUALIZATION

Certainty/Comfort

Uncertainty/Variety

Significance

Love and Connection

Growth

Contribution

One of my mentors from afar, the great Tony Robbins, helped me to truly understand how a lot of our foundation for our actions are based in our basic 6 human needs, and our awareness and self-actualization of them.

I see it all the time, in the sports world and out-people can equate their net worth with their self worth. Their identity is married so deeply to their bank statements and game stats that they've forgotten that money is simply a vehicle for trying to meet our needs, almost all of which are not financial. We're all familiar with the cliche that money cannot buy happiness, but I'm convinced that almost everybody has to learn that lesson the hard way because let's face it; the idea of having enough money to throw at your problems until they're solved is a seductive impulse.

It certainly was something I constantly thought about as a kid. Growing up, money was always out of reach. It was always a source of stress because there was never enough of it. Then, when I changed my perspective, I found joy in serving and giving. Once I start serving and being committed to something bigger than myself and my immediate needs, my value raised, and money along with the strategy to make it, came! . I'd learned the joy of giving and to this day I consider contribution to be one of the six most important things every person needs.

Whatever emotion you're after, whatever vehicle you pursue—being the greatest athlete, building a business, getting married, raising a family, traveling the world—whatever you think your life's mission is, there are six

basic, universal needs that make us tick and drive all human behavior. Combined, they are the force behind the crazy things (other) people do and the great things we do. ;) We all have the same six needs, but how we value those needs and in what order, determines the direction of our life.

Need 1: Certainty/Comfort

The first human need is the need for Certainty. It's our need to feel in control and to know what's coming next so we can feel secure. It's the need for basic comfort, the need to avoid pain and stress, and also to create pleasure. Our need for certainty is a survival mechanism. It affects how much risk we're willing to take in life—in our jobs, in our investments, and in our relationships. The higher the need for certainty, the less risk you'll be willing to take or emotionally bear. By the way, this is where your real "risk tolerance" comes from.

Need 2: Uncertainty/Variety

Let me ask you a question: Do you like surprises? If you answered "yes," you're kidding yourself! You like the surprises you want. The ones you don't want, you call problems! But you still need them to put some muscle in your life. You can't grow muscle—or character—unless you have something to push back against.

Need 3: Significance

We all need to feel important, special, unique, or needed. So how do some of us get significance? You can get it by earning billions of dollars, or collecting academic degrees—distinguishing yourself with a master's or a PhD. You can build a giant Twitter following. Or you can go on The Bachelor or become the next Real Housewife of Orange County. Some do it by putting tattoos and piercings all over themselves and in places we don't want to know about. You can get significance by having more or bigger problems than anybody else. "You think your husband's a dirt bag, take mine for a day!" Of course, you can also get it by being more spiritual (or pretending to be).

Spending a lot of money can make you feel significant, and so can spending very little. We all know people who constantly brag about their bargains, or who feel special because they heat their homes with cow manure and sunlight. Some very wealthy people gain significance by hiding their wealth. Like the late Sam Walton, the founder of Wal-Mart and for a time the richest man in America, who drove around Bentonville, Arkansas, in his old pickup, demonstrating he didn't need a Bentley—but of course, he did have his own private fleet of jets standing by.

Significance is also a money maker—that's where my dear friend Steve Wynn has made his fortune. The man who made Las Vegas what it is today knows people will pay for anything they believe is "the best," anything that makes them feel special, unique or important, anything that makes them stand out from the crowd. He provides the most exclusive, luxurious experiences imaginable in his casinos and hotels—they are truly magnificent and unmatched in the world.

Need 4: Love & Connection

The fourth basic need is Love and Connection. Love is the oxygen of life; it's what we all want and need most. When we love completely we feel alive, but when we lose love, the pain is so great that most people settle on connection, the crumbs of love. You can get that sense of connection or love through intimacy, or friendship, or prayer, or walking in nature. If nothing else works, you can get a dog.

These first four needs are what I call the needs of the personality. We all find ways to meet these—whether by working harder, coming up with a big problem, or creating stories to rationalize them. The last two are the needs of the spirit. These are more rare—not everyone meets these. When these needs are met, we truly feel fulfilled.

Need 5: Growth

If you're not growing, you're dying. If a relationship is not growing, if a business is not growing, if you're not growing, it doesn't matter how much money you have in the bank, how many friends you have, how many people love you—you're not going to experience real fulfillment. And the reason we grow, I believe, is so we have something of value to give.

Need 6: Contribution

Corny as it may sound, the secret to living is giving. Life's not about me; it's about we. Think about it, what's the first thing you do when you get good or exciting news? You call somebody you love and share it. Sharing enhances everything you experience.

Life is really about creating meaning. And meaning does not come from what you get, it comes from what you give. Ultimately it's not what you get that will make you happy long term, but rather who you become and what you contribute will.

Now think about how money can fulfill the six human needs. Can money give us certainty? You bet. Variety? Check. Obviously it can make us feel important or significant. But what about connection and love? In the immortal words of the Beatles, money can't buy you love. But it can buy you that dog! And it can, unfortunately, give you a false sense of connection because it attracts relationships, although not always the most fulfilling kind. How about growth?

Money can fuel growth in business and in learning. And the more money you have, the more you can contribute financially.

But here's what I truly believe: if you value Significance above all else, money will always leave you empty unless it comes from a contribution you've made. And if you're looking for significance from money, it's a high price to pay. You're looking for big numbers but it's unlikely you'll find big fulfillment.

The ultimate significance in life comes not from something external, but from something internal. It comes from a sense of esteem for ourselves, which is not something we can ever get from someone else. People can tell you you're beautiful, smart, intelligent, the best, or they can tell you that you are the most horrible human being on earth—but what matters is what you think about yourself. Whether or not you believe that deep inside you are continuing to grow and push yourself, to do and give more than was comfortable or you even thought possible. The wealthiest person on earth is one who appreciates.

1. Which of these six needs do you tend to focus on or value the most?

2. What are the ways (good and bad) you meet these needs? For example, in your relationships, work, eating, exercise, etc.?

3. How can you increase your focus on growth and contribution? What are some things you can do, or new experiences you can participate in?

Set aside 30 minutes to an hour to read the <u>Self-Actualization Assessment</u> in the back of the workbook in The Appendix.

A crucial step in knowing who you are, is also being aware of how you react and respond emotionally. "To be aware is to be alive."

Self-Awareness

Emotional Self-Awareness is noticing and being able to label your feelings, emotions, "gut-level" instincts or reactions; being able to connect these to their source; recognizing their effects on your mind and your body; using your feelings as a valuable source of insight and information about yourself, others and the situations around you.

When you are Emotionally Self-Aware you are in control of you! It puts you back in the driver's seat of your reactions, your decisions, how you feel and think of yourself, and how you feel and react to others. To be Aware is to be alive! You can't make your highest impact and change in the world until you first discover and become aware of who "you" are! Self-Awareness is key to being SELF Fit™ and is the foundation for your Athletic Identity. Emotions aren't bad. We all have them and are all wired to express them- whether it be outwardly or internal suppression (which later explodes anyway!). The key to impulse control, anger management, better decision making is first to be aware of how you react and why. People with Emotional Self-Awareness are able to:

- Know which emotions they are feeling and why
- Realize, in the moment, the links between their feelings and what they think, do and say
- Recognize how their feelings affect their performance
- Are able to articulate their feelings and appropriately express them
- Can tell – in the moment – when they are getting upset

When you refuse to become emotionally unaware, it not only affects you internally, it also affects your game and performance. Some of the symptoms that you are not Emotionally –Self Aware are that you:

- May receive messages from their bodies such as chronic headaches, lower back pain, neck or shoulder pain, heart racing, sweaty palms, anxiety attacks or other signals, but generally don't pay attention to these signals or connect them to their source, to what's causing these physical symptoms
- Fail to gain insight and information from what their bodies might be trying to tell them
- Get irritated, frustrated or angry easily, causing them to treat people in an abrasive way
- Fail to see that what they are doing or being asked to do might not be aligned with their personal goals and values
- Often feel stressed and out of balance in terms of their work life, health and family

If this is you, don't fret, just develop. Here are a few development tips to help you become more Emotionally Self-Aware of yourself:

- Regularly check in on your feelings. During the course of the day, schedule brief but frequent check–ins on your emotional state as well as what your body might be feeling or trying to tell you
- If you find yourself clenching your teeth, tensing your shoulders, feeling worn out or worn down, stop and ask yourself what your body is trying to tell you – are you feeling strained? Stressed? Anxious? Fearful? Overwhelmed? Discouraged? Burned out?
- Name your emotions and connect them specifically to a source or to a situation, concern, or issue
- "Listen" to what your emotions might be telling you in that moment
- Use the information that bubbles up from inside, listen to your intuition to gain insight that could guide you in dealing with the issue or challenge
- Take the time to be introspective, to listen to that quiet inner voice. Put aside some of your goal-oriented activities and think. Take long walks, know your core values, and especially stop thinking of your emotions as irrelevant or messy. Our emotions are an essential source of valuable information.

What's your story? What story do you live by? What story of yourself do you tell yourself? Is it empowering or discouraging? Does it give you energy or drain the energy out of you? Does it motivate you or inspire you? Does it make you work harder?

The story of The Nobel Peace Prize

Have you ever heard of Alfred Nobel? He was a global arms dealer, who specialized in dynamite, and was pretty successful from doing so. Well, he found out what others thought of his invention when, in 1888, his brother Ludvig died. Though some journalistic error, Alfred's obituary was widely printed instead, and he was scorned for being the man who made millions through the deaths of others. One French newspaper wrote "*Le marchand de la mort est mort*," or "the merchant of death is dead." The obituary went on to describe Nobel as a man "who became rich by finding ways to kill more people faster than ever before."

Nobel was reportedly stunned by what he read, and as a result became determined to do something to improve his legacy. One year before he died in 1896, Nobel signed his last will and testament, which set aside the majority of his vast estate to establish the five Nobel Prizes, including one awarded for the pursuit of peace.

Imagine your funeral and asking what you want your eulogy to consist of, your lifetime achievements to be, the difference you made. What will friends and family say about you? If you have children or plan to one day, what will they say about you? Truthfully, you are writing your eulogy right now every moment, every day right now. Will you end up being just a picture on the wall or the engine that thrust others into a greater future than the one that you once had?

What do you want your obituary to say? Create a Better Story. Create the story that you want to be remembered by. You do this by making emotionally smart and socially responsible decisions. In your relationships, with your finances,

with your team, the way you take care of yourself, the way you handle your responsibilities.

A lot of decisions that you make in life are rooted in your core values. We all have them. The sad thing is that they have often been defined by others, peers, music, TV, and other media. Today, be honest & true to yourself. with yourself become aware of the values that you operate off of and make decisions from currently, and then CHOOSE the values that want to possess and make decisions from moving forwards with your career, life, and relationships. Doing something that contributes to life, adding value to life beyond yourself. Real purpose is always outside yourself, beyond your ego, or your self-interest.

Becoming a solution-oriented Team Player

How do you look at life? Do you see a solution in every challenge or a problem in every circumstance? To make yourself a more solution-oriented team player….

Refuse to Give Up. Thinking about an impossible situation you and your teammates hall all but given up overcoming. Now determine to not give up until you find a solution.

Refocus your Thinking. No problem can withstand the assault of sustained thinking. Set aside dedicated time with key teammates to work on the problem. Make sure it's prime think time, not left over time when you're tired or distracted.

Rethink your Strategy. Get out of the box of your typical thinking. Break a few rules. Brainstorm absurd ideas. Redefine the problem. Do whatever it takes to generate fresh ideas and approaches to the problem.

Repeat the Process. If at first you don't succeed in solving the problem, keep at it. If you do solve the problem, then repeat the process with another problem. Remember, your goal is to create a solution-oriented attitude that you can bring into play all the time.

Do you see a problem in every circumstance or a solution in every challenge?

GRIT, RESILIENCE, and PERSEVERANCE:

What Is Your Pebble?
from *The Pebble in the Shoe*
by Jim Fannin

Some pebbles are of fear. Others are created from guilt, rejection or shame. Maybe not today, but they eventually arrive unannounced and usually at the most inappropriate time. What challenges do they present?

To run the marathon race of life at your most efficient speed, you must be free of embarrassment, guilt, rejection, fear, envy, jealousy, anger, impatience, frustration and worry. All can be lodged in any shoe, from a pair of loafers worn by a city dweller in Manhattan, to a pair of boots on a farm in Montana. These intangible pebbles are crippling. They destroy relationships. They contribute to overeating and gaining unhealthy weight. They coax us into drugs, alcohol and other addictions. They destroy families and alienate friends. They thwart the potential of our children and physically snuff extra years from our life. These are the pebbles in the shoe.

The pebble can cause you to quit or perform with complete indifference. It can help instigate a fight or add disrespectful silence to an otherwise dynamic relationship. Even the desire for fame, fortune or power can turn into a pebble in your shoe if left undetected. Most pebbles stir up the past, cloud the future and keep the present to a blink of the eye. Like a garden that's been freshly tilled, a pebble can reappear without warning or detection. Prevention and removal are your only options for simplicity, balance and abundance.

YOU HAVE TO DEVELOP G.R.I.T!!!!!

GRIT is the tendency to sustain interest in and effort toward very long-term goals (Duckworth et al., 2007). Self-control is the voluntary regulation of behavioral, emotional, and attentional impulses in the presence of momentarily gratifying temptations or diversions (Duckworth & Seligman, 2005; Duckworth & Steinburg). On average, individuals who are gritty are more self-controlled.

People don't see that dealing with "problems" and "challenges" is going to make them healthier and stronger and better as a human being. It's like lifting a weight. The arms strengthen and the weight feels progressively lighter. Dance with challenges until the challenges are too tired to stay any longer. Challenging yourself gives you a relationship that's beneficial. You begin to see it as something that serves you and feeds you and gives you energy and strengths. The more I challenge myself, the less the outside world throws things at me that "look" like obstacles and huge problems that are hard to overcome. The challenges then look easy. Go to the Appendix at the back of the book in the Appendix and take the **GRIT SCALE ASSESSMENT.**

Persevere

to persist in anything undertaken; maintain a purpose in spite of difficulty, obstacles, or discouragement; continue steadfastly

SERVANT LEADERSHIP

What is a a **"Superstar?"** Having GRIT AND excellent SErvant Leadership is what made Magic Johnson not only a superstar but a Great leader and influencer. He figured it out: That whoever wants to be great among you, will serve the most of you. He bought in early. He gave up his stats to make the team better, to win better, to win more. You like the feeling of winning, than the feeling of knowing you had 70 points. A winning mindset...

"Meaning comes from making a Difference. If what you're doing is not making a difference, then it has no meaning."

What are you doing for others? How are you making them better? How are you making your home, your team, your community, the world a better place? And if you're not, what do you plan to start doing to make everywhere that you set your feet…better?

But Jesus called them together and said, “You know that the rulers in this world lord it over their people, and officials flaunt their authority over those under them. But among you it will be different. Whoever wants to be a leader among you must be your servant, and whoever wants to be first among you must become your slave. For even the Son of Man came not to be served but to serve others and to give his life as a ransom for many.”

The Gospel of Matthew

One of my favorite books is "Kingdom Man" by Tony Evans. In the book, Dr. Evans makes an excellent statement. He says that God doesn't care about you being great, that He actually made you to be great; But that your greatness has to be tied and in direct correlation to the capacity that you **serve** and **empathize** with people. This makes all the sense in the world. Let's go a little deeper. Robert K. Greenleaf coined the term **"servant-leadership"** in an essay he first published in 1970, saying:

"The servant-leader is servant first. It begins with the natural feeling that one wants to serve, to serve first. Then conscious choice brings one to aspire to lead. That person is sharply different from one who is leader first, perhaps because of the need to assuage an unusual power drive or to acquire material possessions. The leader-first and the servant-first are two extreme types. The leader who is servant first ensures that other people's highest priority needs are being served."

Robert Greenleaf passed away in 1990, but his principles live on at the Greenleaf Center for Servant Leadership, a non-profit organization that promotes education about servant leadership. The current CEO, Kent Keith, states, —**The simplest way to explain it [servant leadership] would be to say that servant leaders focus on identifying and meeting the needs of others rather than trying to acquire power, wealth and fame for themselves.**

Robert Greenleaf, who spent much of his career in HR and personnel for AT&T, observed over many years that —there were leaders who were in it for themselves and leaders who were in it for others, || according to Keith. And, —his conclusion was that those who focused on others were the most effective leaders. ||
In order to be a servant leader, one needs the following qualities, according to Greenleaf. Many of these are closely related with social and emotional intelligence.

1. **Listening** - Traditionally, leaders have been valued for their communication and decision making skills. Servant-leaders must reinforce these important skills by making a deep commitment to listening intently to others. Servant-leaders seek to identify and clarify the will of a group. They seek to listen receptively to what is

being said (and not said). Listening also encompasses getting in touch with one's inner voice, and seeking to understand what one's body, spirit, and mind are communicating. Do people believe that you want to hear their ideas and will value them?

2. **Empathy** - Servant-leaders strive to understand and empathize with others. People need to be accepted and recognized for their special and unique spirit. One must assume the good intentions of coworkers and not reject them as people, even when forced to reject their behavior or performance. Do people believe that you will understand what is happening in their lives and how it affects them?

3. **Personal Healing + Refreshment** - Learning to heal is a powerful force for transformation and integration. One of the great strengths of servant-leadership is the potential for healing one's self and others. In "The Servant as Leader", Greenleaf writes, "There is something subtle communicated to one who is being served and led if, implicit in the compact between the servant-leader and led is the understanding that the search for wholeness is something that they have." **Do others come to you when their tanks are low and options are few, especially when something traumatic has happened in their lives? Do you do the same?**

4. **Awareness** - General awareness, and especially **self-awareness**, strengthens the servant-leader. Making a commitment to foster **awareness can be scary--one never knows what one may discover!** As Greenleaf observed, "Awareness is not a giver of solace—it is just the opposite. It is a disturber and an awakener. Able leaders are usually sharply awake and reasonably disturbed. They are not seekers of solace. They have their own inner serenity." **Do others believe you have a strong sense of clarity and keen insight into what is going on? Self, Social, and team wise?**

5. **Persuasion + Influence** - Servant-leaders rely on **persuasion, rather than positional authority in making decisions. Servant-leaders seek to convince others, rather than coerce compliance.** This particular element offers one of the clearest distinctions between the traditional **authoritarian** model and that of servant-leadership. The servant-leader is effective at building consensus within groups. **Do others follow up on your requests because they want to, or because they have to?**

6. **Conceptualization** - Servant-leaders seek to nurture their abilities to **"dream great dreams."** The ability to look at a problem (or an organization) from a conceptualizing perspective means that one must think beyond day-to-day realities.

Servant-leaders must seek a delicate balance between conceptualization and day-to-day focus. **Do others contribute their ideas and vision for the good of the group when you are around?**

7. **Foresight + Discernment** - Foresight is a characteristic that enables servant-leaders to understand lessons from the past, the realities of the present, and the likely consequence of a decision in the future. It is deeply rooted in the intuitive mind. Do others have confidence in your ability to anticipate the results of decisions and their consequences? Do people trust you? What is your integrity like? Do you follow-through?

8. **Stewardship-** Robert Greenleaf's view of all institutions was one in which CEO's, staff, directors, and trustees all play significant roles in holding their institutions in trust for the greater good of society. Do others believe you are preparing them to make a positive difference in the world?

9. **Commitment to the Growth of People-** Servant-leaders believe that people have an intrinsic value beyond their tangible contributions as workers. As such, servant-leaders are deeply committed to a personal, professional, and spiritual growth of each and every individual within the organization. Do people believe that you are committed to helping them learn, grow and develop as a whole person?

10. **Building Community** - Servant-leaders are aware that the shift from local communities to large institutions as the primary shaper of human lives has changed our perceptions and has caused a feeling of loss. Servant-leaders seek to identify a means for building community among those who work within a given institution. Do people feel a strong sense of community in the places where you lead?

Servant leaders have a natural desire to serve others. This "calling" to serve is deeply rooted and value-based. Servant leaders have a desire to make a difference for other people as they journey through this life, and they pursue opportunities to impact others' lives for the better. A servant leader is willing to sacrifice self-interests for the sake of others.

Do people believe that you are willing to sacrifice self-interest for the good of the group?

What's your Why?

What happens to us when we think success and money are all we ought to go for? We find that there's nothing there when we get there. There's nothing there. There is no real security in that type of security. There's no comfort in that type of comfort. It becomes fresh, new paranoia. Your Vision, Your "Why" have to be the force that drives you in life. Your family, your love ones, the underdogs in life, the voiceless, THAT have to drive you! Everything that you do in life, every decision that you make should get permission from your vision. And if it don't line up with your "WHY" then it should get dismissed with the quickness.

Your Why comes from Your Hurt, Your Heart, and Your Help. These are the 3 ways that people will connect with you.

Your Hurt:

Your hurt is your pain, your past, those experiences that give you the fuel to keep going. Your "why" is rooted in the things that disgust you the most. The things that you have personally lived through. I have personally been emotionally obese and socially unfit. I know how it feels to be in a bad, unhealthy relationship. I know how it feels to appear successful on the outside and on your bank statement, but are emotionally & relationally bankrupt on the inside.

Your Heart:

Your heart is based from your pain. Your heart is what you care about. Those things and causes that you want to make a difference and impact in. I choose to only work with people that want to make an impact on the lives of others. I truly believe that if your vision came from above that it will, and must include developing and empowering others. If someone doesn't know their vision, it's my purpose to help them pull it out. Your heart is your concerns, your passion that burns deep within.

Your Help:

Your help is what you want to offer. Your solutions. The goal is to not just become a role model. Those are replaceable. The goal is to become a resource that is invaluable. I truly believe that God placed a piece of eternity in each of us that is priceless and immeasurable. That, .y friend, is what you offer the world.

Exercise: Based on the definitions above, defined you "Why":

My Hurt

____

____

____

____

My Heart:

____

____

____

____

My Help:

____

____

____

____

Your "why" is intertwined with your Vision. Your "Why" actually births your vision.

Your vision is developed from your "why." Your dreams and goals should all come from your "Why."

A vision shows up on the inside to show you what's possible on the outside. You can (and should) have a vision for your family, yourself, your relationships, your business and career, your spiritual growth and development, and your health. Bringing your vision from your mind to reality will take work and consistency. But count the costs. The Vision has its own set time to manifest. The value is in the preparation and the process. Don't sweat the small stuff that happen along the way.

There will be discouraging times when it looks like nothing is happening or that your vision isn't even in sight. Keep moving towards it until you can see it clearly. It's all about perspective. You will hear me say this a lot. Perspective is always key. Ask yourself, "do I cry over spilled milk? Or do I just clean it up and keep moving, knowing that I could get some more, or that maybe that carton was spoiled anyway? Perspective can and will be the difference maker and momentum keeper. Your perspective has to have a focal point, and that focal point is your vision. Can you stay big picture focused when storms come? When unfortunate situations occur? When circumstances happen that are out of your control?

A vision gives purpose to actions and helps make decisions when you reach those forks in the road. And trust me, you will reach several forks in the road. Stay the course. You don't have to react to everything, but do have to respond, even if that response is the decision to be silent. What are you holding on to that is keeping you from truly immersing yourself in your vision and purpose? Is it an identity? Is it a reputation? Is it pride? Is it the past? How is what you're holding on to helping you live out your purpose and make your greatest impact on this side of the ground? Please…Please…Live!

FOCUS

You've got to maintain focus under all circumstances. Whether it's the competition trying to break your composure, or you're hurting from fatigue or the conditions are unfavorable, you must stay focused. A winning mindset is teachable.

Similar to the physical part of the game, it'll be easier for some athletes and take more effort from others. But it's not a birthright. A winning mindset is something you practice and train for.

With a winning mindset you possess the capability of willing yourself to win. Instead of caving into the pressure, you'll rise up to the challenge because you trained for those high pressure moments. Focus your attention on solutions, know your strengths, and use your winning mindset to bring out the fearless competitor within.

Every decision in your life is controlled by your beliefs and values. You may not realize it, but you have the power to choose what you believe about your life, people, money and health. You can either choose beliefs that limit you, or beliefs that empower you to move toward success. Your beliefs energize you to create the world you want to live in right now. The key is to be aware of them because what you value determines what you focus on.

Every decision you make, everything that you do, rather it be personal or career wise, should have to get permission from your "Why" first! Let your "why" and your "vision" be your focus point.

"Forward's the Only Direction...On to the Next One.."
–Jay-Z

Never give up...Never Give up...Never give up! As simple as this advice sounds, what you just read was one of the last speeches that Winston Churchill gave in his life. He got up in front of the audience those words, and walked off. Considering all of the times this man had accomplished in his life and all of the wisdom which he shared with the audience, he chose only those 3 words. Why? Because he probably learned that the leading cause of "failure" in any endeavor was the decision to accept *failure* by giving up. Every negative circumstance carries with it the opportunity to learn, to become a better athlete and person, and press on towards the achievement of your dreams. Considering this, it's easy to understand that the only way to truly "fail" at something is to fail to learn, to fail to grow and fail to press on. Giving up is failure. Everything else is simply the opportunity to develop the skills which will eventually lead to success. Stay focused and stay resilient. Constantly

develop your emotional resiliency and your mental toughness. It's a life long journey. Every problem carries with it seeds which you can plant towards the achievement of your goals and becoming your true athletic self. Every seemingly negative situation in your life is there to teach you, test you, and motivate you. If you continue to learn, grow, and to persist, you will eventually develop the status of "Great."

Focus on your present. Focus on the moment that you are in. Focus on executing that moment perfectly. Then, by default, your future will be great. Many people never get what they want out of life because they never determine what they really want. CHOOSE who and what you want to be! A laser beam is nothing more than light which is focused towards one central point. Light can brighten a room, but "focused" light can cut through steel! Focus...

THE POWER OF SELF-DISCIPLINE

Author H. Jackson Brown Jr. quipped, "Talent without discipline is like an octopus on roller skates. There's plenty of movement, but you never know of it's going to be forward, backwards, or sideways." If you know you have talent, and you've seen a lot of motion-but little concrete results-you may lack self-discipline.

Sort Out Your Priorities. Think about which 2 or 3 areas of life are most important to you. Write them down, along with the disciplines that you must develop to keep growing and improving in those areas. Develop a plan to make the disciplines a daily or weekly part of your life.

List The Reasons. Take the time to write out the benefits of practicing the disciplines you've just listed. Then post the benefits someplace where you will see them daily. On the days when you don't want to follow through, reread your list.

Get Rid of Excuses. Write down every reason why you might not be able to follow through with your disciplines. Read through them. You need to dismiss them as the excuses they are. Even if a reason seems legitimate, find a solution to overcome it. Don't leave yourself any reasons to quit. Remember, only in the moment of discipline do you have the power to achieve your dreams.

A nursery in Canada displays this sign on its wall: "The best time to plant a tree is twenty-five years ago…The second best time to plant a tree is today." Plant the tree of self-discipline in your life today.

"Whatever your hand finds to do, do it with your might…."

10 Tips to help you Perform at your highest Potential

1. **Let Go of what others think-** Some people will be positive, and some people will not- that is a constant

2. **Perform for yourself, not to impress or "not disappoint" others-** Remember your "Why" and perform with that in mind

3. **Accept that you will make mistakes, and let them go-** Perspective is everything. Learn from them

4. **Focus on what you can control**

5. **Recognize when you are using negative self-talk and replace it with positive-** You always have a Choice- Which report will you believe?

6. **Rather than performing perfectly, perform to see improvement-** Always be thinking, "How can I get better…"

7. **Be objective about your game, not subjective-** What would you say to your best friend if they performed like you did? Don't treat yourself worse!

8. **Focus on the Journey, not the destination**

9. **Celebrate Your successes-** Your hard work paid off. Take a moment to reflect on it, pat yourself on the back, and get back to work!

10. **Stay in the moment**- The only moment you have control over is the present one. What will worrying about the next one benefit you?

Mentally tough leaders never take these 13 actions.

All world class athletes are physically strong. But it's mental toughness that determines whether an athlete claims, and holds, the #1 spot. Like an Athlete, you've got to keep your head in the game when the pressure is on. These actions were developed by my friend Dr. Loren

13 actions mentally tough leaders never take:

1. **Feel sorry for yourself.** Self pity is a waste of time. It depletes your power. Sure there are bad calls by referees, injuries at critical moments and unexpected upsets. Life's not fair. Seek the insights instead of the problems. Then take personal responsibility to make necessary changes to be better prepared next time.
2. **Become powerless.** Don't allow anyone else to define who you are or how you should feel. Insecure athletes give away their power. Recognize that you ALWAYS have total control over your feelings and your actions. Don't let anyone tell you otherwise.
3. **Avoid change.** It's easy to get comfortable and stop pushing yourself. Mentally tough athletes consistently seek to push beyond their current abilities. That's because complacency is the enemy. Continually strive to do more, be more and achieve more.
4. **Dwell on things beyond your control.** It's not what happens to you that matters most. It's your response that determines your mental toughness. Only two things lie within your control: your actions and your attitude. Everything else is a test to determine how well you maintain focus under pressure.

5. **People pleasing.** Bullies and people pleasers share a common quality. Both are indicators of low self esteem. Here's where boundaries do matter. Know how to be a team player. Even more important, know when to take a stand for what you believe in.
6. **Avoid all risk.** Risk averse individuals rarely rise to the top. Their resistance to judgment or criticism from failure causes them to stick with known outcomes. Risk assessment is a learned skill which quickly measures the pros and cons of a move.
7. **Re-live past mistakes.** Things happen. Nothing good comes from reliving a past mistake over and over. It's done and you can't change that. Now it's time to focus on the present, and then work toward a better future. Acknowledge past mistakes, gain insight from them and then make the necessary changes for a better outcome next time around.
8. **Repeat history.** Close minded athletes continually make the same mistakes. Their ego is preventing them from seeing what's really happening. Laying blame and making excuses is a poor strategy. Feedback improves self awareness, and mistakes are a primary source of feedback.
9. **Envy.** Resentment, envy and jealousy are common emotions that arise when other athletes win. Mentally tough leaders take a different stance. They see those successes as a sign of what's possible. And trust that their dedicated efforts will contribute to a similar pay-off.
10. **Quit too soon.** Obstacles and blocks will occur. Here's where your response matters. You'll define yourself by the failure if you quit too soon or allow the opportunity to slip away. Mentally tough leaders know that if you're not failing then you're not trying hard enough. Failure is a critical stepping stone for breakthrough performance.
11. **Avoid time alone.** Some individuals avoid time alone. There's a difference between loneliness and solitude. Don't depend on others for your happiness. Solitude offers the opportunity to reflect, recharge and release.
12. **Entitlement.** Don't make the mistake of taking your talent for granted. That's because one day you'll face an opponent who's determined to claim your spot. Entitlement and complacency go hand in hand. Mentally tough leaders

understand the value of putting in the time and effort. That's because there's very limited competition for leaders who put extra effort.

13. **Seek immediate gratification.** Quick fixes, magic bullets and instant celebrity are an illusion. Top athletes dedicate years of effort to achieve their BIG vision. Greatness takes time. The success mindset aligns your long term vision, with your values. Vision and values determine your actions.

Mentally tough leaders seek to win...

You're not expected to be perfect. It takes dedicated effort to reach the top.

It's easy to become impatient. Mentally tough leaders aim beyond immediate gratification. They accept that greatness takes time. So they're willing to put in the effort and prepare for the next opportunity.

Challenge: Know what you truly care about. What's most important to you? List your motives, goals and vision. Identify how you're mentally tough. Now identify which beliefs help you to be mentally tough. Describe a time when you rose up to the challenge. List the strategies which keep you focused on the BIG picture. Now you know where you stand on these things. Finally, list how you want to be in the future.

Challenges and obstacles are your friend. The hunger drives you to the next level. Make them your employee. Make them work for you. How do you grow a muscle. Stretch it. Add weight. It has to be conditioned.

"The Legs Feed the Wolf!"

Build your core and your legs. They will provide the strength to keep going, the strength to be mentally tough. The strength to be "emotionally fit and socially responsible in the game of life!"

Core strength: your heart.

Leg Strength: Your Actions and making the step.

How bad do you want to be the best you and make your biggest impact in the world?

Understanding Mental Blocks for The Leader & How to Manage Them

Mental blocks are sometimes the big unknown. There is no other thing that dries out an leader's joy faster, drives a coach to insanity, or confuses a parent more, than having an athlete, a child, or their self experiencing a mental block.

A mental block, as I use it here, is a fear response to a skill or skills that a leader has previously been able to perform without problems. There are multiple reasons for a "block". Before I get into those, I want to explain something first. Before conceding yourself to believe you have a block, make sure it is in fact, a block. Say for example if an athlete has not been able to perform a skill to near perfection, in a multitude of venues, it is in fact, not a block. In those instances, you can take a deep breath and overcome the troubling situation by taking one step back and making sure that the athlete has learned proper progression. There is no need to compound the situation, by giving it a name or diagnosis that doesn't actually name the struggle that the athlete is having. Here's an example for an Athlete, but applies to all:

There are many reasons why a leader experiences a mental block. The first, is that an athlete has been injured, had a near miss, or has seen someone else get hurt. Another reason, is that the leader is plagued by stress inside their arena. where they no longer feel control. Typically unconsciously, the leader is trying to control an environment, because they do not feel control anywhere else. A third reason, is that the leader learned skills too quickly and without proper progression. Their mind finally caught up to their body and they realized- "Whoa! What am I trying to do here?" They then become paralyzed, questioning their ability and their own safety. There are many other "reasons" why an individual experiences a mental block, but there are the main reasons I have seen in my experience of working with those in leadership.

The good news is that there is help and there are people- world class & average athletes, high achievers to beginners out there every day that are

overcoming these blocks. But be warned, it is not an easy process. There is not a quick fix, but there have been proven methods that have assisted athletes through these blocks and help them catapult themselves back into competition.

7 Key Tips to Manage a Mental Block

1. Change Your Environment

When you notice fear creeping in-whether it's a sensation in your body or a thought in your head, attempt to relax your mind or your body. If you ar unable to slow yourself down, change your environment. To do this, helps your mind to recalibrate. To continue standing there for endless minutes, only solidifies your body's fear response and ends up flooding your ability to cope.

2. So Something New!

If you have been blocked for some time, try something different, unless you've found something that has worked. If you know that when you stand in front of the mirror, you get scared, stop standing in front of the mirror. If you are intimidated by a coach, let them know, and then try to cater and individualize their talks to you.

3. Visualize

When you are in a relaxed state, visualize yourself being able to perform that skill again. What do you notice happening to your breath? Your body? Your thoughts? In this environment, try to bring yourself back down to a relaxed state. Work on your positive affirmations and feel the changes that are occurring in your body as you say those positive things to yourself.

4. **Be Kind to yourself**

What you are going through is a difficult hurdle. You have hurdles like this throughout your life. Be forgiving and kind to yourself. Think: What would I tell a friend or loved one if he/she was going through something similar? It's interesting how we are much more patient and understanding to others who are going through a difficult time.

5. **Be Aware of the Cues/Sensations of your Body**

Be aware of the cues/sensations in your body: Our bodies, when presented with a fearful event, will either go into flight, fight or freeze mode. This usually happens before our minds even have a chance to tell us why we are responding the way we do. To understand your tendency to fight, flight, or freeze, will help you be aware of what may be happening to your body when fear creeps in. Knowing how your body reacts to fear provides you the most helpful tool in how to overcome this seamlessly automatic response.

6. **Harness the power of Relaxation**

The most powerful tool you can have in your tool belt is the ability to create a relaxed state. Being in the moment and aware of your breathing will help you get to a place where you can relax your mind and your body. Your mind is not capable of fear, when your body is relaxed. In that state, your body understands, and fear is no match for understanding! If you can assist your body in relaxing, your mind will follow. "Where the mind goes, the body will follow." And vice versa.

7. **Positive Affirmations**

Create positive cues; "I can do it." "Relax," "I'm capable," I know how to do this," "Trust myself"

It's all about Attitude

"The longer I live, the more I realize the impact of attitude on life. Attitude, to me, is more important than facts. It is more important than the past, the education, the money, than circumstances, than failures, than successes, than what other people think or say or do. It is more important than appearance, giftedness or skill. It will make or break a company…a church…a home…a school. The remarkable thing is we have a choice everyday regarding the attitude we will embrace for that day. We cannot change our past…we cannot change the fact that people will act in a certain way. We cannot change the inevitable. The only thing we can do is play on the one string we have, and that is our attitude. I am convinced that life is 10% what happens to me and 90% how I react to it. And so it is with you…we are in charge of our Attitudes."

–Charles Swindoll

Never... Ever...

Ever...

STOP...

DREAMING!!!

NOTES

NOTES

NOTES

NOTES

NOTES

NOTES

NOTES

NOTES

About the Author

Jemiah Battle, aka Mr. EQ, is founder of The SELF Initiative, an Emotional fitness trainer, and certified life coach specializing in EQ, identity development, leadership development, and social & life transitions. This book is based on the tested, results-focused strategies that he uses daily with private clients and in his own life and relationships. He believes in real world Solutions for real world people. Jemiah is a sought after keynote speaker and media contributor. He students, ypung professionals, coaches athletes, celebrities, and high achievers in becoming emotionally fit, mentally tough, and socially responsible. He lives in Greenville, SC with his wife Renea, and has two kids. Jaheim & Maji.

You can follow him at:

www.Facebook.com/JemiahBattle

www.Twitter.com/MrEQfitness

Instagram @MrEQfitness

To learn more about him and his initiatives visit WWW.JemiahBattle.com

To bring a Blue Print for Mental Toughness™ or Resiliency, or GRIT Workshop or Symposium to your University,College, School, Conference, or Organization, please send an email at <u>Info@TheSELFinitiative.com</u> and also visit www.JemiahBattle.com

Appendix

Appendix I: Self-Actualization Scale for Needs Assessment

Self-Actualization Scale For Needs Assessment (SASNA)

Needs Analysis Scaling Tool

Developed by
L. Michael Hall, Ph.D.
and Tim Goodenough

Executive Summary

The Matrix Embedded Hierarchy of Human Needs is a Neuro-Semantic model developed from the work of Abraham Maslow and his Hierarchy of Needs model. This model expands Maslow's original work making it more dynamic and alive. As it does this, it enables us to understand, recognize, and work with *human driving needs.* We are a needy species. Biologically we are animals and Maslow strongly recommended, —Be a good animal; have healthy appetites. || Needs are simply *the requirements for life and for effectiveness.* As you learn to effectively understand your needs and cope with them, you move on to the next level of development. This is the first requirement for self-actualization— having a healthy biological foundation with sufficient physical energy, emotional energy, and personal (or —spiritual ||) energy.

As a strength-based model the Needs Assessment tool enables you to look at yourself (or another person) through the eyes of human strengths and potentials. It enables you to identify strengths, talents, and resources that can be tapped and more fully utilized for self-actualization. The following tool provides a way to use the Hierarchy of needs for *needs Assessment* for coaching and training in service of self-actualization.

This Self-Actualization Needs Assessment Tool is designed to answer the question that Tim asked that originated this tool, —How can we use the Hierarchy of Needs for facilitating and enabling self-actualization? || And self-actualization means being —the best you || that you can be, it means finding and unleashing your highest values and visions and your best performances and achievements. And this allows you to be —fully

alive, fully human. || It means *being* what you are and when you do, you are authentic, congruent, and alive with integrity.
As an assessment tool, you should be able to do the *first level analysis* by yourself. For deeper analysis, we recommend that you ask a Certified Meta-Coach to facilitate the process with you.

How to think about and Use the Assessment Tool

1) Start at the bottom and work up.

Begin with the survival needs and work up the diagram. The diagram of the pyramid is made up of many continua of needs, several in each category (survival, safety, social, and self). Use the framework of each line as a continuum that measures your *overall, global, or general sense of efficiency in meeting your needs.* How are you doing? What is your overall sense? Are you getting by? Then you are in the middle. If you are *not quite getting by,* there's some stress and strain in getting your needs met effectively, then you are on the left side—in the Red Zone. If you are not only getting by but doing pretty good, then you are to the right of the middle, in the Green Zone.

2) Think of the continuum as a measurement of your overall coping with your driving needs.

The continuum goes from the far left side and gauges several stages in the process of handling your needs: dysfunction, distortion (coping is at extremes of too much, too little), not quite getting by. The Red Zone is where the *deficiency needs* are crying out that you are just not satisfying/ gratifying the needs well. You are either not using —true gratifiers || (Maslow) or the gratification is too much, too little (the —extremes) or completely distorted and creating all kinds of human dysfunction— neurosis and psychosis.

The continuum on the right side of the middle gauges the stages beyond —Getting by: || getting by pretty well, doing very good, optimizing your coping skills (having some expertise in them), to maximizing them (being absolutely masterful in handling them). No one is completely at the right hand of the continuum. —Masters || can move there from time to time. It is the ideal of where you can reach in terms of effectively gratifying your needs. When there, your consciousness, emotions, and energies are completely freed from that driving need so that you have all of that available for moving up the hierarchy and into the human self-actualizing needs at the top.

Dysfunctional Extremes Not Getting By Getting By Getting by Doing Good Optimizing Maximizing
Neurotic Too much Cravings, Doing Ok Well - Thriving Super-Thriving At one's very
Psychotic Too Little Dissatisfaction Normal concerns Feeling Good Best

3) Mark your default point and your range.

Without identifying any particular context, answer it globally or generally for your life. (We will use various contexts later). Put a check (or tick) where you basically are today. Then put brackets [around where you move back and forth— the range of your coping gratifications]. The check is your default point (use one color for this). The brackets is your range (use a different color for this).

4) Sort for quantity and Quality.

As you think about gratifying each need —note the amount (number, volume, quantity) of how many gratifications there are for the need. Then note the quality of those gratifications. Indicate Quantity (amount, times, how often, degree, volume, etc.) with a —V || (for volume) and for Quality use a —Q.

5) At the top identify your highest life themes, visions, and meanings.

Above the —lower needs(the animal needs, Maslow) are the —higher || or human needs. These self-actualization needs is where you truly live the *human life.* Here you can live for contribution, justice, fairness, music, beauty, mathematics, making a difference in a given area, health, spirituality (as you define it), excellence, honor, loving, etc. What do you live for? What is the highest meaning and vision of your life? What do you seek to actualize? Identify 3 of your top ones and put them in the three circles at the top.

Deepening the Analysis

By using the *Needs Analysis Tool* you can achieve numerous degrees of analysis, depending on how deep you want to do a needs analysis with yourself or a client. You can use the Hierarchy Needs Analysis in numerous levels to go deeper and deeper with each new layer of analysis. A Meta-Coach can facilitate this for a deep analysis.

1) *First Analysis:* First use the tool to get a general picture of your coping skills as you gratify the basic human needs that drive you. Here are essential questions to ask after you complete the diagram:

Where are you overall?

How are you gratifying your needs? Doing what? How coping?

Do you live in the Red Zone mostly or in the Green Zone mostly?

Is there a particular level of need (survival, safety, social, or self) that you could address that would provide a real unleashing of potentials?

What have you discovered from this first level analysis? What are you aware of?

Are there any strong areas of deficiency?

Are there any strong areas of optimizing or maximizing that gives you a real resource?

Is there any need that you are not gratifying effective that's serving as an interference to your self-actualization?

Did you leave any of the need continuums blank? Why?

The relationship between Volume— Quality in fulfilling your needs: Notice where you put the V and the Q for each need:

Is the Quality always beyond (and higher) than the Volume?

Is the Quality always before (and lower) than the Volume?

Do the Q and the V shift around depending on the need?

Is the Quality and the Volume always or usually together?

2) *Second Analysis:* Next explore your (or another person's) thinking, understanding, believing, deciding, etc. that sets up the standards of evaluation that you or the other person uses:

What do you think or believe about X? (Any continuum need)

How accurately do you judge your thinking and understanding about X?

What evaluations have you heard from others about need X?
What does it mean to you to —get by? How do you feel about that?
How stressful is it when you are not —getting by?
How stressful is it when you are in the Red Zone?

3) *Third Analysis:* Another analysis can be around the thinking style used to create and evaluate the need and ways of coping with it. Examine the thinking and evaluating by the list of Cognitive Distortions to detect to what extent they play a role in how you think and cope:

Cognitive Distortions Advanced Cognitive Styles

1. Over-generalizing Contextual thinking
2. All-or-nothing thinking Both-and thinking; in-between thinking
3. Labeling Reality-testing thinking
4. Blaming Responsibility thinking
5. Mind-reading Current sensory information
6. Prophesying Tentative predictive thinking
7. Emotionalizing Witness thinking or non-emotionalizing
8. Personalizing Objective thinking
9. Awfulizing Meta-cognitive thinking
10. Should-ing Choice thinking
11. Filtering Perspective thinking
12. Impossibility thinking: Can't-ing Possibility thinking
13. Discounting Appreciative thinking
14. Identifying E-prime / dis-identifying thinking

4) *Fourth Analysis:* For this analysis, imagine yourself —in the shoes of someone who knows you very well. || Now fill out a second Pyramid Assessment *from that second-position perspective*
How does that compare to your first Assessment?
What insights or awareness does this give you?

5) *Fifth analysis:* Another level of analysis that you can use is that of contexts. If you use a specific context: work and career, home, relationship, hobby, sports, leadership, management, etc., then what new or different information emerges?
What contexts are important to you? Identify one and fill out the Needs Analysis again using that context.
What new awarenesses or insights does this elicit for you?

The Diagram of Needs —

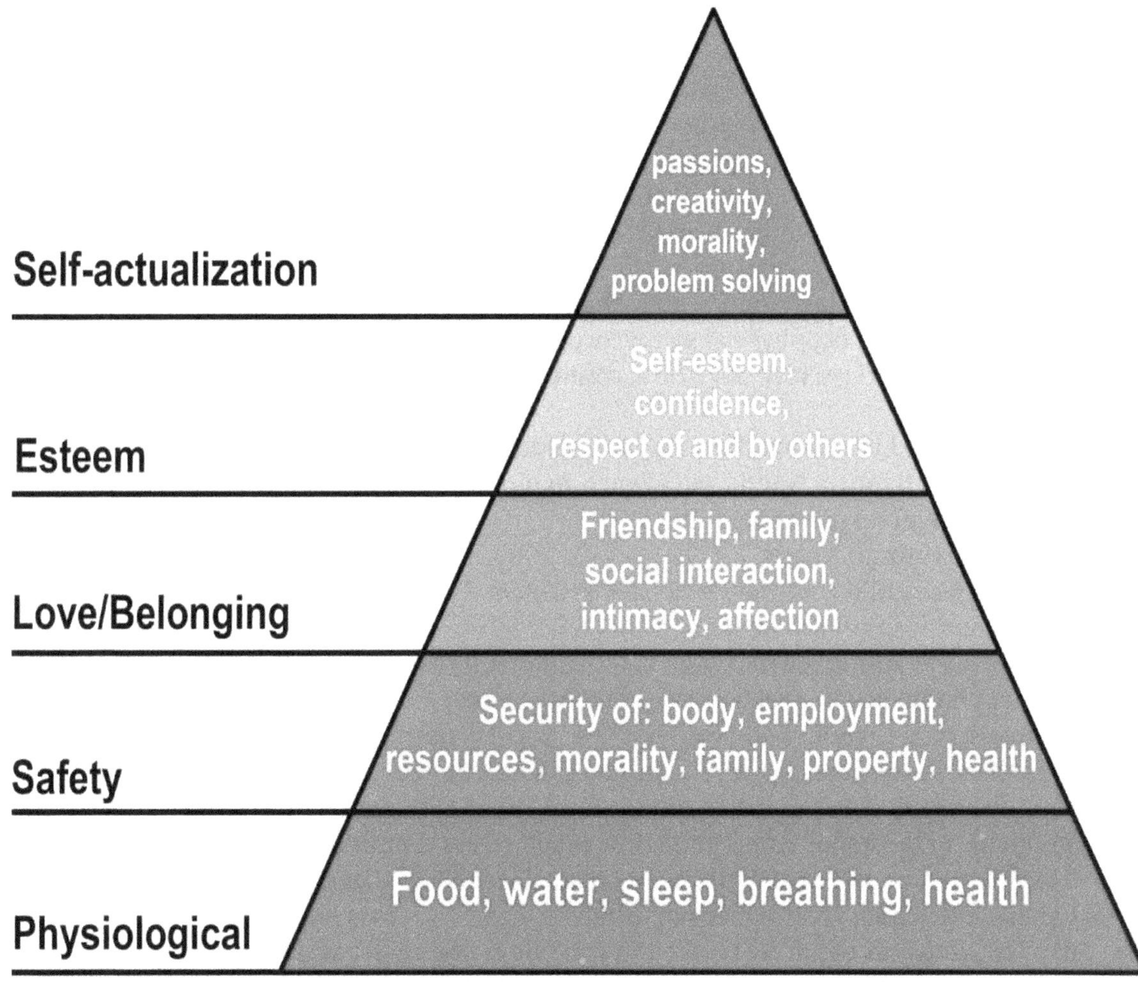

Some Background for Understanding the Hierarchy of Needs

Maslow organized human *needs* using a hierarchical structure that is known as the Hierarchy of Needs. These include the following. The first group of four are the lower needs, the animal needs— the higher intelligent animals have these needs as we do. These are driven by *deficiency* —by lack. When you do not adequately gratify them, the deficiency creates energy, motivation, emotions, etc. leading to coping behaviors. When they are gratified, the drive goes away. The higher needs are the growth needs that make us truly human and are not driven by deficiency at all. The better the gratification, the more the drive grows and increases. These make a person richer, fuller, and more self-actualizing.

1) **Survival Needs**: List: food, water, shelter, clothes, money, pro-creative sex.
2) **Safety Needs**: List: physical safety, order, structure, control.
3) **Social Needs**: List: love, affection, connection, bonding, part of a group, approval, acceptance.
4) **Self Needs**: List: importance, dignity, value, worth, respect, status, honor.
5) **Self-Actualization Needs**: excellence, exploration, contribution, legacy, justice, fairness, democracy, wonder, etc.

Exploring Human Needs

After you have filled out the *Pyramid Assessment Tool,* you can use it to explore in more depth your needs or the needs of a client.

1) *Health and Vitality.* Identify the health and vitality of each need: What healthy and what level of vitality do you feel with regard to this need?
1) How strong is your need or drive for X? 0 to 10, how intense?
2) Is the drive or need at a level that you can handle? How dominating is it?
3) How often do you think about your drive/ need? (Hourly, daily, weekly, monthly)
4) Do any of the needs stress you? How much stress does it create for you?
5) Does the way you gratify the need create a leash? How does it leash you and prevent you from reaching your higher potentials?
6) What activates the drive or need in you? How does it get amplified?
7) How do you experience it?
8) Are your coping skills able to effectively gratify your needs and leave you with energy and vitality for the purpose of your life?

2) *Meanings:* Identify the meanings informing and governing each need:
1) What do you think about need X? [X being any of the needs]
2) What do you believe about the need and what do you believe about your coping behaviors?
3) What is your criteria and standards for making the evaluation about it that you did?
4) Do you experience or seek to experience —the meaning of life || through any of the lower needs? If so, which one? (Example, money, status, friends, acceptance, etc.)
5) At what level do you find yourself most frustrated?
6) What need level do you feel stuck at? Which seems to prevent you from going after your dream and unleashing your highest and best?

3) *Semantic overloading.* Identify if there is any semantic overloading of meaning creating distortions of the need:
1) Is there any need that you have given *too much meaning*? Too much importance? If so, which one?
2) Is there any need that you have given *too little meaning*? If so, which one?
3) Do you have any limiting beliefs about that need? Has anyone suggested that you might?
4) How much of your mental and emotional time do you think about that need?
5) Do you engage in psycho-coping behaviors? (Psycho-eating, psycho-spending, psycho-sexing, psycho-saving, etc.)
6) Are you facing any negative behavior consequences from your eating, exercising, earning, saving, relating, etc.? (example: health problems, relationship, career problems)
7) What happens to your needs under some/moderate stress?
8) What happens to your needs under major stress?
4) *Contexts:* Explore the semantic environment around the need:
1) What are your meanings and beliefs about the context of any given need?
2) In what contexts do you thrive?
3) In which contexts do you just get by and need more effective ways of coping?
4) In which contexts do you struggle to even get by meeting your needs?
5) *Skills:* Explore your skills for gratifying (satisfying) the needs:
1) With any given need, how do you gratify this need? How else?
2) How effective are you in these coping skills?
3) Which skills need improving or changing? Which are excellent?
4) How extensive is your repertoire of skills for gratifying any given need?
5) What are your very best skills in meeting your needs?
6) How often do you use your coping skills to satisfy the drive or need? How often do you forget to use them?
6) *Peak Experiences:*
1) Have you and do you still hear your true voice? What is it? What message summarizes the highest value and vision in you?
2) Do you express your true voice? How true are you to your inner calling?
3) How often do you experience peak experiences? (Daily, weekly, monthly)
4) What are your five highest self-actualizing needs?
5) What do you feel that you were born to do? How much have you actualized that today?
6) Now that you know your strengths and resources for unleashing potentials, what does that open up for you?
7) How else could you use your strengths to unleash more potentials?

End Notes

1) You can find Maslow's best work in *Toward a Psychology of Being* (1965) and *Motivation and Personality* (1954; 1970). And you can find the Neuro-Semantic models that have extended and expanded Maslow's work in *Unleashed!* (2007), *Self-Actualization Psychology* (2008), and *Unleashing Leadership* (2009). Also see www.self-actualizing.org. Neuro-Semantic trainers and coaches (Meta-Coaches) are part of a new Human Potential Movement focused on *actualizing excellence in individuals and organizations.* See www.neurosemantics.com.

2) The Neuro-Semantic models that expand and extend Maslow's original work are the following.

The Self-Actualization Quadrants: Based on the axes of meaning and performance.

The Matrix Embedded Pyramid of Needs: Based on the hierarchy of needs and the Matrix Model of Neuro-Semantics (2002). This turns the pyramid into a volcano of energy enabling a person to find and actualize his or her highest and best.

The Self-Actualization Matrix: A matrix of meaning frames that develops self-actualization in terms of its meaning, intention, and state as well as self-actualization for one's identity (self), capacities (powers), relationships (others), time, in different domains (world).

3) The Hall / Goodenough Self-Actualization Scale for Needs Assessment is designed for as a tool for Meta- Coaches, a tool for identifying where a person is strong and skilled in meeting the basic human needs that drive us and where a person may need coaching. The Scale enables you to identify areas that will facilitate the unleashing of potentials.

Appendix II: Your CORE Values Assessment

Your values are your GPS navigation system for life. Getting them defined and properly calibrated is one of the most important steps in redirecting your life toward your grandest vision. The below series of questions will help you evaluate and refine what is truly important to you and what matters most in life. Answer each question thoughtfully, and then I will help you select the top half-dozen values for your life.

Who is the person I respect most in life?

____

What are their core values?

____

Who is my best friend, and what are his/her top three qualities?

____

If I could have more of any one quality instantly, what would it be?

____

What are three things I hate? (e.g., cruelty to animals, credit card companies, deforestation, etc.)

____

Which three people in the world do I dislike the most and why?

____

Which personality trait, attribute or quality do people compliment me on the most?

____

What are the three most important values I want to pass on to my children?

____

If I were to teach a graduating high-school class values that would give them the best opportunity for success in life, what would those be and why?

____

If I had enough money to retire tomorrow, what values would I continue to hold? What values do I see being valid 100 years from now?

____

The top dozen qualities of the "ideal" man or woman relationship:

____

Now take a look at your answers above. Do you notice any re-occurring themes? Taking what you've observed in others, what others have observed about you, what you want for others, and things you would fight for or against, create a list of your top 10 values (in any order) below.

Top 10 Values:

1.
2.
3.
4.
5.
6.
7.
8.
9.
10.

Now, let's reduce it down to the half-dozen most important to you. Put a star by the values you're sure about. Then take the ones you feel are important but aren't sure if they're top-six material and put them in pairs. Think about two of those values side by side, and ask yourself which of the two is more important, eliminating the other. Keep pitting the survivors against each other until you're down to six. If some of the values you listed are just two words describing the same idea, combine them.

Top 6 Values:

1.
2.
4.
5.

3. 6.

Now prioritize your core values in order of importance, with the most important first. All are important, of course, but which are the most important? If you had to choose between two values, which would you fight for, or even die defending? Now which are your top three?

MY TOP 3 VALUES IN LIFE ARE:

1.

2.

3.

Sample Values

Abundance| Alertness| Ambition| Anticipation| Appreciation| Assertiveness| Attentiveness| Audacity| Awareness| Balance| Acceptance| Accountability| Accomplishment| Accuracy| Achievement |Acknowledgement| Adaptability |Adventure| Alertness| Ambition |Anticipation |Appreciation| Assertiveness |Attentiveness| Audacity| Awareness| Balance| Beauty| Belonging |Blissfulness |Boldness| Bravery| Brilliance |Calm |Candor |Carefulness |Caring |Certainty| Challenge |Change |Charity| Cheerfulness Clarity |Cleanliness| Collaboration| Longevity| Love| Loyalty |Love Making a difference| Mastery| Maturity| Comfort| Commitment| Communication| Community| Compassion Competence| Competition| Concentration| Confidence |Connection |Consciousness |Consistency Contentment| Content |over fluff Continuity| Continuous Improvement |Contribution| Control |Conviction |Convincing |Cooperation Courage Courtesy| Creativity Curiosity Daring Decisiveness Delight |Dependability| Desire |Determination| Devotion Dignity |Diligence| Discipline Discovery Discretion| Diversity |Drive |Duty |Eagerness |Education| Effectiveness| Efficiency| Elation| Elegance |Empathy |Encouragement |Endurance |Energy |Enjoyment| Enthusiasm |Equality| Excellence |Excitement |Experience|Expertise| Exploration |Expressiveness| Fairness| Faith |Fame |Family |Fidelity| Flexibility |Flow| Focus| Forgiveness |Fortitude |Freedom| Friendship| Frugality |Fun Generosity |Giving| Going the extra mile| Goodness| Grace| Gratitude| Growth| Guidance |Happiness |Harmony |Hard work| Health |Helpfulness| Heroism| Holiness| Honesty| Honor |Hopefulness Hospitality| Humility| Humor| Imagination| Independence| Influence| Ingenuity| Inner peace| Innovation |Insightfulness| Inspiration| Integrity |Intelligence| Intensity| Intimacy| Intuitiveness| Inventiveness| Investing| Joy |Justice| Kindness |Knowledge |Leadership| Learning Liberty| Logic |Meaning| Merit |Mindfulness|

Modesty |Money |Motivation| Nonviolence| Openness| Opportunity| Optimism| Order |Organization| Originality |Outcome |orientation| Outstanding service| Passion| Peace |Perceptiveness| Perseverance |Persistence| Personal growth |Pleasure|Poise |Positive-attitude| Power| Practicality |Precision |Preparedness| Presence |Preservation |Privacy |Proactive |Progress| Prosperity| Punctuality |Quality| Quiet| Rationality| Recognition| Relationships |Reliability Religion Resourcefulness| Respect |Responsibility |Righteousness |Risk-taking |Romance| Safety| Security |Selflessness Self-esteem |Seriousness| Service |Simplicity| Sincerity |Skill |Speed |Spirit |Stability |Strength| Style Systemization| Teamwork |Timeliness| Tolerance |Tradition |Tranquility| Trust |Truth| Unity |Variety |Well-being |Wisdom

Appendix III: GRIT SCALE ASSESSMENT

The G.R.I.T. Scale

Directions for taking the Grit Scale: Please respond to the following 12 items. Be honest – there are no right or wrong answers!

1. I have overcome setbacks to conquer an important challenge.
   - Very much like me
   - Mostly like me
   - Somewhat like me
   - Not much like me
   - Not like me at all
2. New ideas and projects sometimes distract me from previous ones.*
   - Very much like me
   - Mostly like me
   - Somewhat like me
   - Not much like me
   - Not like me at all
3. My interests change from year to year.*
   - Very much like me

- Mostly like me
- Somewhat like me
- Not much like me
- Not like me at all

4. Setbacks don't discourage me.
    - Very much like me
    - Mostly like me
    - Somewhat like me
    - Not much like me
    - Not like me at all
5. I have been obsessed with a certain idea or project for a short time but later lost interest.*
    - Very much like me
    - Mostly like me
    - Somewhat like me
    - Not much like me
    - Not like me at all
6. I am a hard worker.
    - Very much like me
    - Mostly like me
    - Somewhat like me
    - Not much like me
    - Not like me at all
7. I often set a goal but later choose to pursue a different one.*
    - Very much like me
    - Mostly like me
    - Somewhat like me
    - Not much like me
    - Not like me at all
8. I have difficulty maintaining my focus on projects that take more than a few months to complete.*
    - Very much like me
    - Mostly like me
    - Somewhat like me
    - Not much like me
    - Not like me at all
9. I finish whatever I begin.
    - Very much like me

- Mostly like me
- Somewhat like me
- Not much like me
- Not like me at all

10. I have achieved a goal that took years of work.
    - Very much like me
    - Mostly like me
    - Somewhat like me
    - Not much like me
    - Not like me at all
11. I become interested in new pursuits every few months.*
    - Very much like me
    - Mostly like me
    - Somewhat like me
    - Not much like me
    - Not like me at all
12. I am diligent.
    - Very much like me
    - Mostly like me
    - Somewhat like me
    - Not much like me
    - Not like me at all

Scoring:

1. For questions 1, 4, 6, 9, 10 and 12 assign the following points: 5 = Very much like me 4 = Mostly like me 3 = Somewhat like me 2 = Not much like me 1 = Not like me at all

2. For questions 2, 3, 5, 7, 8 and 11 assign the following points: 1 = Very much like me 2 = Mostly like me 3 = Somewhat like me 4 = Not much like me 5 = Not like me at all

•

Add up all the points and divide by 12. The maximum score on this scale is 5 (extremely gritty), and the lowest scale on this scale is 1 (not at all gritty).

Duckworth, A.L., Peterson, C., Matthews, M.D., & Kelly, D.R. (2007). Grit: Perseverance and passion for long-term goals. Journal of Personality and Social Psychology, 9, 1087-1101.

Appendix IV:The Resilient Mind & Changing your Mindset

The Resilient Mindset In order to become or remain resilient, it's important to understand our own thoughts, feelings, and behaviors. Do they contribute to our resilience or make it more difficult? Once we understand how our thoughts, feelings, and actions impact us, we are better able to make positive changes.

Thinking That Hinders a Resilient Mindset

Check the ones that you believe apply to your thinking. Think about what you can do differently to change the behavior or thinking pattern. Do you engage in . . .

- Filtering: Do you take the negative details and magnify them while filtering out all positive aspects of a situation?
- Polarized Thinking: Do you have a tendency to look at things as black or white, good or bad? For example, do you tend to think you have to be perfect or you're a failure? That there is no middle ground?
- Overgeneralization: Do you come to a conclusion based on a single incident? If something bad happens, do you expect it to happen over and over again?
- Mind Reading: Do you tend to make assumptions about what people are feeling and why they act the way they do? Do you tend to divine how people feel about you?

- Catastrophizing: Do you expect the worst? Do you tend to anticipate disaster? Do you notice or hear about a problem and immediately start to think about the "what ifs? "What if tragedy strikes?" "What if it happens to me (or my family, etc.)?"
- Personalization: Do you have a tendency to think that everything people do or say is some kind of reaction to you? And do you tend to compare yourself to others, trying to determine who's smarter, better looking, earns more, etc.?
- Control Fallacies: Do you tend to feel you are controlled by external circumstances? If so, you are helpless, a victim of fate. On the other hand, do you tend to feel immense internal control? If so, you feel responsible for the pain and happiness of everyone around you. Both are control fallacies. What's realistic?
- Fallacy of Fairness: Do you feel resentful because you think you know what is fair and right but other people don't agree with you?
- Blaming: Do you hold other people responsible for your pain and struggles, or take the other tack and blame yourself for every problem or reversal? Neither thought pattern supports a resilient mindset.
- Shoulds: Do you have a list of rules about how you and other people should act? Do people who break the rules anger you? And do you feel guilty when you violate the rules?
- Fallacy of Change: Do you expect other people to change to suit you if you "help them" enough? Is it possible you feel that people need to change because your happiness seems to depend on them?
- Being Right: Do you continually try to prove that you are right? Is being wrong unthinkable? Do you tend to go to any length to demonstrate your "rightness"?
- Heaven's Reward Fallacy: Do you expect all your sacrifice and self-denial to pay off, as if there was someone keeping score? Do you feel bitter when the reward doesn't come

Changing Your Mindset Exercise

Write examples of your behavior in these situations and how you can change it to support a more resilient mindset.

- Worrying about situations you can't control
- Failing to see choices, or having "tunnel vision"
- Being a "professional procrastinator"
- Expecting perfection of yourself and/or others

- Resisting change through inflexibility and rigidity
- Turning all situations into competitions where someone has to win and someone has to lose
- Focusing on faults rather than strengths, or being self-critical
- Failing to set limits or say "No"
- Taking poor care of yourself (not getting enough sleep or poor eating habits, stopping exercise, drinking/smoking more when stressed.)
- Expecting all problems should be neatly resolved What's the one behavior you think you can start working on changing right away? How will you do that?

APPENDIX V: Building Your Vision Worksheet & Defining your Associations

"Leaders take charge, make things happen, dream dreams and then translate them into reality. Leaders attract the voluntary commitment of followers, energize them, and transform organizations into new entities with greater potential for survival, growth and excellence. Effective leadership empowers an organization to maximize its contribution to the well-being of its members and the larger society of which it is a part. If managers are known for their skills in solving problems, then leaders are known for being masters in designing and building institutions; they are the architects of the organization's future."

- Burt Nanus, 1994

Throughout history, great leaders have been those who could develop a clear, elevating and compelling vision, one that attracts commitment, inspires people, revitalizes organizations, and mobilizes the resources needed to turn vision into reality. There is no more powerful engine for driving an organization forward toward excellence and long-range success than an attractive, inspiring, worthwhile, achievable vision of the future, widely held. There's an old Chinese proverb that says that unless you change direction, you are likely to arrive at where you are headed. Is your current direction desirable? Will it get you and your organization where you want to go? Where you need to go? This worksheet is designed to help you think through your vision – a vision for yourself in your own professional life, as well as a vision for the organization you are leading. Quite simply, a vision is a realistic, credible, attractive future for you and for your organization. It is your articulation of a destination toward which you and your organization should aim, a future that is better, more successful, or more desirable than is the present. Our founding fathers, for example, wrote the Constitution to describe their vision for the United States. It set forth a clear direction and defining values, but did not specify how to get there. Here are a few guidelines for creating a vision statement for your organization:

A vision articulates a future state of being. It should describe a standard of excellence, an ideal, for what an organization will be one year, three years, or five years from now. It bridges the present and future.

- A great vision should be inspiring, motivating, and elevating. It should attract commitment and energize people. In 1961, John F. Kennedy's vision was to put a man on the moon by the end of the decade. His vision inspired the nation. It was motivating, uplifting and succinct (a plus). It also set out a timeframe. Martin Luther King's I Have a Dream speech is one of the most uplifting, inspiring, energizing visions ever. A vision often calls for sacrifice and emotional investment, and creates meaning in people's lives.

- It should clarify purpose and direction. A great vision is persuasive and credible in defining what the organization wants to make happen, and creates aspirations for people in the organization. It focuses the organization's agenda and priorities.
- It should be ambitious and establish a standard of excellence. A great vision compels people to want to do a good job and helps them see how they can effectively advance the organization's purpose. It must be seen as a stretch from where the organization is currently. It should expand the organization's horizons.

- It should be memorable, vibrant, and visual; it should paint a picture in people's minds of what is possible. Pictures transform words into mental models that people can carry around in their heads. Your vision should create an image or picture that will transform words into something tangible in people's minds.

- A vision can be a few sentences or a few paragraphs – probably longer than JFK's one-line vision, but shorter than MLK's I Have a Dream speech. It should be well articulated, unambiguous and easily understood. Try to keep it short, however. You want to communicate it to others in three-to-five minutes. Any longer than that, and your audience may begin to lose interest.

- It must reflect your values, what's important to you, what you feel passionate about. Vision always deals with the future. Indeed, vision is where tomorrow begins, for it expresses what you and others who share the vision will be working hard to create. Since most people don't take the time to think systematically about the future, those who do – and who base their strategies and actions on their visions – have inordinate power to shape the future. This worksheet has been designed to help you shape your future.

"Those who envision greatness usually achieve it"

–Carl Larson

1: Define Your Personal Vision

An author who traveled to over 100 different countries privately conducted an unscientific survey of many of the people he met in his travels. One of his questions was, "What's the most important thing in life to you?" The answer he received over and over was, "I want my life to count. I want to make a difference." In preparing to define your personal vision, reflect on the following questions and jot your answers in the space provided: My "Big Purpose" in Life: Define what you see as your primary purpose in life. In your reflections, consider:

- What originally attracted you to this line of work?

- What makes you feel passionate about what you are doing?
- What is the single most important accomplishment for you to achieve in your lifetime?
- What difference do you want to make in this world?
- What do you see as your life's work?
- What do you want to be most remembered for accomplishing?
- What do you need to have accomplished at the end of your time to be able to look back and say, "I am truly proud of what I've done with my life"?

Step 2: Clarify Your Values

Values comprise those concepts and ideas that are most important to us. They are deep-seated, pervasive standards that influence almost every aspect of our lives: our moral judgments, our responses to others, our commitments to personal and organizational goals, and how we go about our work and relate to one another. Values powerfully influence thinking and action in the organization and, ultimately, the choice of vision. Here are a few examples of values:

- The ultimate job of management is to serve the front line employees delivering the service, not the other way around. Management should work to eliminate barriers that impede front-line excellence, not create them.
- Risk-taking in the name of innovation is encouraged in this organization; mistakes are seen as a fair price to pay for learning and innovation.
- We do business through honest and truthful dialogue; there is no recrimination for straight talk.
- People at all levels of the organization respect the fact that there is life beyond work. List your values below; values that define who you are as an individual and as a leader:

1. ____

2. ____

3. ____

4. ____

5. ____

6. ____

7. ____

8. ____

9. ____

10. ____

Step 3: Define Your Vision for Your Team or Organization

A distinguished philosopher once wrote that the greatest force for the advancement of the human species is "a great hope held in common" (Teilhard de Chardin, 1959). Selecting and articulating the right vision for your organization is the toughest task and truest test of great leadership. Your Team's or organization's vision should reflect its core purpose, its reason for being. It should reflect the idealistic motivations that drive people to do the organization's work. Ideally it should capture the heart and soul of the organization.

The Core Purpose of This Team

Define what you see as your Team's or Organization's core purpose. As you reflect, consider these questions:

- What value does your team or organization provide to society?
- What is your team's unique position in the industry?
- What does success look like for your team?
- What are your values and the values held by other key individuals in your team?
- Who are your most critical and most important stakeholders?
- What are their major interests and expectations?

Step 4: Communicate Your Vision

A vision is little more than an empty dream until it is widely shared and accepted. Only then does it acquire the force necessary to change an organization and move it in the intended direction. The key to communicating your vision is connecting with people in a meaningful way to encourage them to embrace a new perspective about what is important and why. The key to gaining widespread commitment to a new vision is to present it in such a way that people will want to participate and will freely choose to do so. This certainly can't be done through coercion or manipulation, but rather through ongoing and regular conversations with people as active partners and colleagues in the enterprise, discussing the vision in terms that address their own legitimate and idealistic interests and concerns. It means connecting with people in a way that resonates with their own deepest feelings about what is right and worth doing. In communicating their vision, leaders form their intentions with full knowledge of the aspirations and values already existing in the organization and then merge the resulting vision with the existing mental framework of each individual team member – individuals and leadersinside the organization, as well any other important people outside the organization. This is accomplished by ensuring your message is communicated regularly, frequently and consistently, ensuring your vision is clear to everyone with whom you come in contact, and particularly the employees within the organization.

To help them avoid distractions and increase their productivity, team members must understand not only what they should be doing, but how their work supports the bigger picture and why it's important to the success of the organization. Communicating your vision is critical to its implementation. It is through dozens and dozens of conversations that leaders use their time to influence and direct their workforce, to build relationships, networks and organizational focus. Communicating your vision can motivate and inspire new levels of commitment and achievement in your organization. Effective leaders invest a great deal of time in networking with people both inside and outside the organization to generate trust and consensus for their vision.

Assessing Your Current Associations as regards to Your Vision

This is about the amount of TIME you spend with people outside of your immediate household (parents, siblings, spouse and kids) and your strict work interactions (those at school, those on your team, or those in your office). Evaluate their level of success in each of the areas below.

Name/ Physical/ Financial /Business/ Profession Mental/ Attitude Spiritual/ Loving/ Family /Relationships/ Lifestyle

Average= 1. 2. 3. 4. 5. =Above Average

Now, organize your associations into the following three categories: dissociations, limited associations and expanded associations.

Disassociations

Maybe you need to disassociate from someone in the chart above, or anyone else who is involved in your life to any degree, who has a negative influence on you—mentally, emotionally, attitudinally, physically or otherwise. These are people who have a negative effect on what you talk about, what you eat, drink, do, watch, listen to, etc.

1.

2.

3

Limited Associations

Who do you spend a significant amount of time with that you might need to pull back from a bit? They are a good person, but they aren't necessarily going where you want to go. They don't have the same ambition, drive and goals as you do in life. Too much time with them might keep you stagnant, or worse, drag you down a bit.

1.

2.

3.

Expanded Associations

Based on your goals and the person you want to become, who do you need to be around more often? Who in your expanded sphere of influence can you find a way to spend more time with?

1.

2.

3.

Mentorship

Additionally, consider where you can hire a coach, trainer or mentor to reinforce your accountability and accelerate your growth rate. You can also find mentors in books, CD programs, seminars, and also at TheSELFinitiative.com.

Appendix VI: 5 Components for Personal Growth

As any farmer knows, the growth of a crop only happens when the right ingredients are present. To harvest plentiful fields, the farmer has to begin by planting the right seed in rich topsoil where sunlight and water can help the seed to sprout, mature, and bear fruit. If any of the ingredients (seed, topsoil, sunlight, water, etc.) are missing, the crop won't grow.

Growing as a person also requires the proper ingredients. Unless the right attitudes and actions are cultivated you will sputter and fail rather than growing in influence. Let's look at 5 basic qualities essential for personal growth.

1. **Teachability**- Arrogance crowds out room for improvement. That's why humility is the starting point for personal growth. As Erwin G. Hall said, "An open mind is the beginning of self-discovery and growth. We can't learn anything new until we can admit that we don't know everything already." Adopting a beginner's mindset helps you to be teachable. Beginners are aware that they don't know it all, and they proceed accordingly. As a general rule, they're open and humble, noticeably lacking in the rigidity that often accompanies experience and achievement. It's easy enough to have a beginner's mind when you're actually a beginner, but maintaining teachability gets trickier in the long term especially when you think you have already achieved some degree of success.
2. **Sacrifice**- Growth as a leader involves temporary loss. It may mean giving up familiar but limiting patterns, safe but unrewarding work, values no longer believed in, or relationships that have lost their meaning. Whatever the case, everything we gain in life comes as a result of sacrificing something else. We must give up to go up.
3. **Security**- To keep learning throughout life, you have to be willing, no matter what your position is to say, "I don't know." It can be hard to admit lacking knowledge because you may feel as if everyone is looking to you for direction, and they don't want to let people down, however, most people aren't searching for perfection, they're looking for an honest, authentic, and courageous individuals who, regardless of the obstacles facing them will

keep working and won't rest until the situation is solved. One must be secure enough to keep taking the stage and honing your skills until you can connect. Being insecure, listening to negative evaluations of others, will seal your fate and you will not excel.

4. **Listening**- Listen, learn, and ask questions from somebody successful who has gone on before you borrow from their experiences so that you can avoid their mistakes and emulate their triumphs. Solicit feedback and take to heart what you're told. The criticism of friends may seem bitter in the short-term but, when heeded, it can save you from falling victim to your blind spots.
5. **Application**- Knowledge has a limited shelf life. Unless used immediately or carefully preserved, it spoils and becomes worthless. Put the lessons you learn into practice so that your insights mature into understanding.

"It is necessary to try to surpass one always; this occupation ought to last as long as life."

–Christina, Queen of Sweden

Appendix VII: Learned Optimism

(From Learned Optimism, by Martin Seligman, Ph.D.)

If you hang your mental response to adversity, you can cope with setbacks much better. The main tool for changing your interpretations of adversity is disputation. Practice disputing your automatic interpretations of events. When you find yourself down or anxious or angry, ask what you are saying to yourself. Sometimes the beliefs will turn out to be accurate; when this is so, concentrate on the ways you can alter the situation and prevent adversity from becoming disaster. But usually your negative beliefs are distortions.

Challenge them.

Don't let them run your emotional life. Learned optimism is easy to maintain once you start. Once you get into the habit of disputing negative beliefs, your daily life will run much better and you will feel much happier.

Let's begin.

Create an ABC record

A = adversity, B = belief, C = consequence.

Example 1: A. You and your significant other have a fight. B. You think "I never do anything right." C. You feel (or do) ________________________________

Example 2: A. You and your significant other have a fight. B. You think, "She (or he) was in an awful mood." C. You feel (or do) ________________________________

Example 3: A. You and your significant other have a fight. B. You think, "This is a misunderstanding, and I am good at clearing up misunderstandings." C. You feel (or do)

____

In the first example, you think, "I never do anything right." (permanent, pervasive, personal) You might feel depressed or sad and not try to do anything to heal the breach. If, as in the second example, you think, "He was in an awful mood". (temporary and external) You will feel some anger, a little dejection, and only temporary immobility. When the mood clears, you'll probably do something to make up. If, as in the third example, you think, "I can always clear up misunderstandings," you will act to make up and you soon will feel pretty good and full of energy.

Keep an ABC diary for the next day or two, just long enough for you to record five ABCs from your own life. To do this, tune in on the perpetual dialogue that takes place in your mind. "Adversity" can be almost anything – a leaky faucet, a frown from a friend, a crying baby, a large bill, inattentive spouse. Be objective – just record our description of what happened, not your evaluation of it. So if you have an argument with your spouse, you might write down that he was unhappy with something you said or did. Record that. But do not record, "he was unfair" under "Adversity" – that's an inference and should be recorded under "Belief." Your beliefs are how you interpret the adversity. Be sure to separate thoughts from feelings. Feelings go under "Consequences." "I feel incompetent" is belief and can be evaluated. "I feel sad" expresses a feeling. It doesn't make sense to check the accuracy of "I feel sad" – if you feel sad, you are sad. In the "Consequences" section record our feelings and what you did. Did you feel sad, anxious, joyful, guilty, or whatever? Often you will feel more than one thing. Write down as many feelings and actions as you are aware of. What did you then do? "I had no energy," or "I made a plan to get him to apologize," or "I went to bed" are all consequent actions.

Over the next couple of days, record five ABC sequences from your life. Use the space given page (and get scratch paper if necessary):

Belief:

Consequence:

Adversity:

Belief:

Consequence:

Adversity:

Belief:

Consequence:

Adversity:

Belief:

Consequence:

Adversity:

Belief:

Consequence:

When you have recorded your five ABC episodes read them over carefully. Look for the link between your belief and the consequences. What you will see is that pessimistic explanations set off passivity and dejection, whereas optimistic explanations energize. The next step follows immediately. If you change the habitual beliefs that follow adversity for you, your reaction to adversity will change. A highly reliable way to change pessimistic beliefs once you are aware of them is to dispute them. Successfully disputed beliefs are less likely to recur when the same situation presents itself again. The most convincing way of disputing a negative belief is to show that it is factually incorrect. Since pessimistic reactions to adversity are so often overreactions, adopt the role of detective and ask, "What is the evidence for this belief?" or "What alternative explanations might there be?"

This is now the ABCDE approach – we are adding two steps – disputing our beliefs and examining the evidence behind them, or seeking alternative explanations. It is important to note the difference between this and the "power of positive thinking." Positive thinking often involves trying to believe upbeat statements such as "Every day, in every way I'm getting better and better." In the absence of evidence, this may be hard to believe. Learned optimism, on the other hand, is about accuracy and examining our negative beliefs. Usually the negative beliefs that follow adversity are inaccurate. Learned optimism works not through an unjustifiable positivity about the world, but through the power of "non-negative" thinking.

So now, I'd like to request you practice the ABCDE method. You already know what ABC stands for. D is for disputation; E is for energization. You will find that in disputing your negative beliefs, you will feel energized and able to take positive action. During the next five adverse events you face, listen closely for your beliefs, observe the consequences, and dispute your beliefs vigorously. Look for evidence to dispute your beliefs. Then observe the energization that occurs as you succeed in dealing with the negative beliefs, and record all of this.

For example:

Adversity: I threw a dinner party to celebrate a new friend's birthday, and she barely touched her food.

Belief: The food was awful. I'm a lousy cook. I might as well forget getting to know her any better. I'm lucky she didn't get up and leave in the middle of dinner.

Consequence: I felt really disappointed and angry with myself. I was so embarrassed about my cooking that I wanted to avoid her for the rest of the night. Obviously, things didn't go as I'd hoped.

Disputation: This is ridiculous. I know the food wasn't awful [evidence]. She may not have eaten very much, but everyone else did [evidence]. There could be a hundred reasons why she didn't eat much [alternatives]. She could be on a diet, she might not have been feeling well, she might just have a small appetite [alternatives]. Even though she didn't eat much, she did seem to enjoy the dinner [evidence]. She told some funny stories, and she seemed to be relaxed [evidence]. She even offered to help with dishes [evidence]. She wouldn't have done that if she was repulsed by me or the food [evidence and alternative].

Energization: I didn't feel nearly as embarrassed or angry, and I realized that if I avoided her, then I really would hurt my chances of getting to know her better. Basically, I was able to relax and not let my imagination ruin the evening for me.

Okay, now you do it in your daily life over the next week. Don't seek out adversity, but as it comes along, tune in carefully to your internal dialogue. When you hear the negative beliefs, dispute them. Beat them into the ground. Then record the ABCDE.

Adversity:

Belief:

Consequences:

Disputation:

Energization:

Great! Now keep going using this format until you have established a new habit of mind.

We Believe In YOU!!!

NOW…

GO CHANGE THE WORLD!!!

www.ingramcontent.com/pod-product-compliance
Lightning Source LLC
Chambersburg PA
CBHW081517040426
42447CB00013B/3254

* 9 7 8 0 6 9 2 4 0 1 5 4 5 *